MOVEMENT AND FUNDAMENTAL MOTOR SKILLS FOR SENSORY DEPRIVED CHILDREN

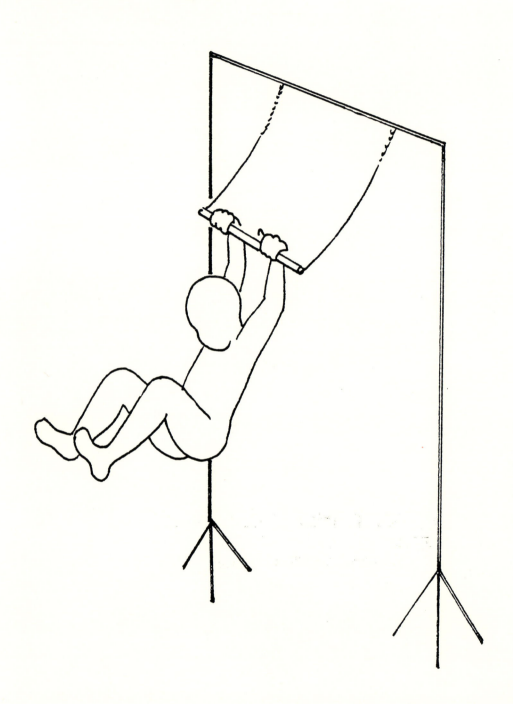

MOVEMENT AND FUNDAMENTAL MOTOR SKILLS FOR SENSORY DEPRIVED CHILDREN

By

LAURA E. KRATZ

Professor Emeritus
Bowling Green State University

LOUIS M. TUTT

Superintendent
Missouri School for the Blind

and

DOLORES A. BLACK

Associate Professor
Bowling Green State University

CHARLES C THOMAS • PUBLISHER
Springfield • Illinois • U.S.A.

Published and Distributed Throughout the World by

CHARLES C THOMAS • PUBLISHER

2600 South First Street

Springfield, Illinois 62794-9265

ISBN 0-398-05392-8

Library of Congress Catalog Card Number: 87-24361

With **THOMAS BOOKS** *careful attention is given to all details of manufacturing and
design. It is the Publisher's desire to present books that are satisfactory as to their physical
qualities and artistic possibilities and appropriate for their particular use.* THOMAS
BOOKS *will be true to those laws of quality that assure a good name and good will.*

Printed in the United States of America
Q-R-3

Library of Congress Cataloging in Publication Data

Kratz, Laura E.
    Movement and fundamental motor skills for sensory
deprived children.

    Bibliography: p.
    Includes index.
    1. Blind-deaf children — Education. 2. Motor learning.
I. Tutt, Louis M. II. Black, Dolores, A. III. Title.
[DNLM: 1. Blindness — in infancy & childhood. 2. Deaf-
ness — in infancy & childhood. 3. Education, Special. 4.
Motor Skills — in infancy & childhood. 5. Movement — in
infancy & childhood. 6. Sensory Deprivation — in infancy &
childhood. WE 103 K896m]
HV1597.2.K73 1987   371.91'1   87-24361
ISBN 0-398-05392-8

PREFACE

WHILE OBSERVING Louis Tutt teaching motor skills to deaf-blind children at the Michigan School for the Blind, I was impressed with the success that he had with his pupils and the joyousness with which he worked and they responded. Since his work has never been published, I took on the project, with his permission, of making his work available for others to use when working with these children.

In order to better understand my task, I read any materials I could find relating to the subject. They are sparse and I had difficulty in documenting them, since many of them were papers presented at American and European seminars, without dates. I spent two years visiting and working with deaf-blind children in several schools.

The text is the result of these efforts on my part, dealing primarily with the movement needs of deaf-blind children in infancy and early childhood, combined with the work of Louis Tutt while teaching at the Michigan School. He wishes to dedicate his material to those 32 deaf-blind children who taught him a lot about teaching, and who are part of the reason that he is where he is today: Superintendent of the Missouri School for the Blind.

In assembling the materials I collaborated with Dolores Black of Bowling Green State University (Ohio), who has for many years directed an activity clinic for handicapped children at that school.

L. E. K.

ACKNOWLEDGEMENTS

I AM INDEBTED to the authorities at Rio Grand Elementary School, Rio Grande, Ohio, and to the schools for the blind in Michigan (Lansing), Ohio (Columbus) and Missouri (St. Louis) for permitting me to observe, question and work with the children and their teachers in the blind, deaf-blind, and multi-handicapped units of their schools.

Dolores Black is responsible for the outline figures demonstrating activities and concepts in the text, with the exception of figures 7-1 and 7-3, which are the work of Lynn McElwee of the Missouri School for the Blind.

The children's drawings of their concepts of their activities are by David and Carolyn, pupils in Tutt's classes in Michigan. The flash card figures were designed by Tutt.

I gratefully acknowledge the critical reading of the text and suggestions made by Patricia Griffith, Coordinator of Deaf Education at Bowling Green State University.

L. E. K.

CONTENTS

MOVEMENT AND FUNDAMENTAL MOTOR SKILLS FOR SENSORY DEPRIVED CHILDREN

CHAPTER ONE

INTRODUCTION

THE TERM "sensory deprived" used in the context of this book refers to children who are deaf-blind and those who have the single handicap of blindness. In the very early years of life the two groups can be taught similarly, using manual body movement, tactile stimulation and imitation. The blind move far ahead in developmental skills later on, with the added advantage of hearing. With deaf-blind children the developmental lag is much greater. Parents and teachers become the focus in the early lives of these children; exposing them to motor activity becomes and remains very important.

Deaf-blind children present a very complicated set of problems. Their double sensory deprivation is so severe, particularly in the very early stages of life, that there are no simple solutions. Without the stimulation of sight and hearing even the reflex movements are greatly diminished. The infant must be stimulated tactually and the body and limbs moved manually to perform the normal movements of rolling over, kicking and grasping. Touch and movement are the primary ways this child will become aware of the environment and the people in it, and perceive of itself as a separate entity from them.

Without movement these children will remain in a state which can only be described as an existence. With movement, they can become whatever their learning potential will permit.

The material presented here is for those who are teaching motor activity to children who cannot hear or see well enough, or are impaired by blindness alone, to function adequately in the everyday world. The task is enormous. It is not, however, impossible. Louis Tutt, a physical education specialist, has proven that success can be achieved in teaching motor skills to deaf-blind children.

The problems of the motor skills teacher are mainly concerned with achievement at very basic levels, and having realistic expectations of accomplishment. It is progressing ever so slowly—slower than can be imagined. It is helping the child achieve the next very small step forward and being pleased with his progress, and it is learning to adapt and adjust one's own feelings and expectations to the situation.

Tutt tells of going from frustration to encouragement and joy in the teaching of these children, once he discovered who they were and the challenges presented by them. Tutt further comments that had it not been for motor activity classes, they would have remained stagnate, doing little and learning nothing. It is necessary for them to learn activity that will help them control their bodies in the future, diminish bizarre behavior, and increase their ability to learn.

The approaches used that make the program succeed are patience, repetition, and consistency. Creativity and imagination are as important, as well as knowing the child through observation and evaluation. All of these play significant roles and all involve the teacher and the parents. Teachers must also join with the physical, occupational and speech therapists in a transdisciplinary approach to put it all together for the child.

Role of the Senses and Sense Deprivation

Doctor Robert J. Smithdas, a deaf-blind adult, has succeeded in being a functional part of society and the world. He states that for the deaf-blind person, " . . . the world literally shrinks: It is only as large as he can reach with his fingertips or by using his severely limited sight and hearing, and it is only when he learns to use his remaining secondary senses of touch, taste, smell and kinesthetic awareness that he can broaden his field of information and gain additional knowledge" (Smithdas 1975).

In the approach to learning presented here, the use of these secondary senses is emphasized, plus the use of any sight or hearing present, to the optimum of potential that exists.

It is chiefly through the senses that the organism mediates between inner needs and external circumstances. The five senses are classified as "close" and "distant" modalities (Myklebust 1964). The distant senses are hearing and vision and the close senses are smell, taste and touch.

Vision is directional, often referred to as spatial, and is primarily a foreground modality. Hearing acts as a background modality, keeping the organism in contact with the environment at all times, encompassing all directions, and in general is referred to as temporal in character.

Sight can be compared to a searchlight beam, sweeping the area, while hearing acts as fog horn, emitting sound into the atmosphere generally.

All infants are dependent on the close senses in early life. The deaf-blind child remains dependent, possibly for his lifetime, on the close modalities, using taction or touch for basic contact and exploration of the environment. Smell or olfaction is not highly developed in human beings; it quickly adapts to a stimulus and ceases to signal the organism of further cognition processing, and taste or gustation is a very limited modality. *Thus, touch, the tactual modality, assumes the lead role in relation to the external environment.*

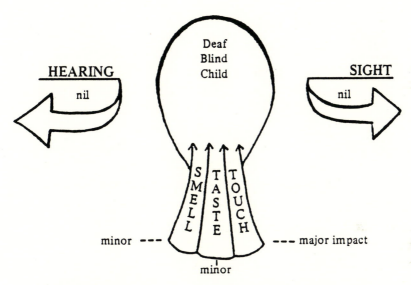

Figure 1-1. Modes of external impact on the deaf-blind child.

Inner needs become and remain foremost in behavioral patterns for the deaf-blind person, while external circumstances, through lack of impact, are virtually ignored. All children have basic inner needs. For normal children, these needs are mediated by circumstances and their environment, such as parental influence, other children, schedules and choice making. Unless the deaf-blind child is made aware of the environment, satisfaction of immediate needs remains primary throughout life. For this reason, the deaf-blind are sometimes selfish, impatient and subject to temper tantrums. Learning to take turns and working with other children and adults as partners help dispel the environmental vacuum.

Characteristics of the Deaf-Blind Child

In the years of infancy and childhood (and perhaps for the rest of their lives) deaf-blind children have problems of isolation and communication that other children do not have. These problems retard their physical, mental and emotional maturation processes. An examination of the characteristics of deaf-blind children (van Dijk 1965) will aid in understanding approaches to teaching them.

They are bound up in their own world so that there are no contacts or relationships with anyone or anything. They are autistic-like. The primary problem is contact with and interest in the outside world. In the beginning, and sometimes for longer periods of time, they are enveloped in their own bodies. They do not know their parents, and some do not know themselves. There is no distance between the world and the child, but rather the child is interwoven with the world of action.

The essence of the teaching task is to bring stimuli to the child through modalities other than sight and hearing, and to set up a system of communication based on tactual signals and cues (Freeman 1975).

They are not motivated by a spontaneous need for moving and they are tactically defensive, i.e., do not like to be touched. In the beginning, movement of the child's body, arms and legs is necessary to stimulate responses. The child must be turned manually from front to back in the crib and arms and legs moved to reach a toy or bottle. If the child is left alone because there is an aversion to being touched, more contributions are being made to retardation in development.

Figure 1-2. Turning the infant manually, front to back. Concepts after figures found in LEARNING STEPS (1976) pp 72, 73, 279, courtesy of the California State Department of Education.

Figure 1-3. Turning the infant back to front, using blanket. Concepts after figures found in LEARNING STEPS (1976) pp 72, 73, 279, courtesy of the California State Department of Education.

They are not interested in doing, seeing or finding out about everything as a normal child is. They are in a lower pattern of behavior, where the outside world only satisfies a very basic need. The child uses objects only as a means of self-satisfaction and self-stimulation. If the child is in a lower pattern of behavior, it is imperative that we elicit movement patterns; otherwise the child will remain in this state. As van Dijk has stated, movement is the only way of learning for this child.

They are not in possession of any real integration of the sensory pathways. Their feelings are undifferentiated and they express themselves in a disorderly way. It is often not clear whether laughing or crying express positive or negative feelings.

They are rarely totally blind and profoundly deaf. There is probably some degree of hearing and some amount of vision. These residual capacities, no matter how slight, will help. Assessment of vision and hearing can be made by simple observation of responses to stimuli when the child reacts in a structured situation.

In the nonverbal child, the lack of language very deeply influences behavior (Magin 1980). More than other stages, this nonverbal stage has its own inner characteristics. The normal child is conscious of the symbolic value of language between the first and second year. The deaf-blind child is five or six, or even older, before grasping the idea of symbols. Some never do.

The body image is nil: They do not know where their arms and their feet are, and have no idea of the size of their bodies. Body image is very important to the child in differentiating between himself and the outside world. Body reference is needed in orientation to locations and to positions in the external environment, such as "up," "down," "back," "under," and so forth. Body knowledge is vital to the development of self-esteem, ego and self-awareness (Magin 1980).

The teaching of fundamental motor skills contributes effectively to the development of body image for the deaf-blind child. Visually impaired children also have problems with self-awareness and body image, particularly with the body in relation to space. The teaching of motor skills is vital to their development, as well. As a matter of fact, all children benefit from instruction in fundamental motor skills to improve body image and self-awareness, but it is particularly important for those with sensory impairments.

CHAPTER TWO

SENSORY IMPAIRMENT DEFINED

THE AMERICAN National Study Committee on the Education of Deaf-Blind Children defines a deaf-blind child as one whose combination of handicaps prevents him from profiting satisfactorily from educational programs for the blind child or educational programs for the deaf child.

The rubella epidemic (German Measles) of 1964-1965 left an estimated 30,000 infants in the United States with one or more of the following: visual defects, auditory defects, cardiac malformations, mental retardation and central nervous system disorders. Hearing loss is the most common manifestation of congenital rubella, and cataracts and glaucoma are the most serious eye defects found in this group. Recent reports have shown that rubella is the leading cause of deaf-blindness in the United States (M. Efron, in Walsh and Holzberg 1981). Usher's Syndrome is the leading cause of hearing and visual impairment among adults. The disease involves a profound loss of hearing and a progressive loss of vision due to retinitis pigmentosa.

Types of Blindness

Legal blindness is defined in the United States as 20/200 vision, or less, after correction. What the normally sighted person sees at 200 feet, presuming he has 20/20 vision, the legally blind individual, at best, must stand within 20 feet to see. At first glance this appears to be an immense figure; on second thought, however, 20/200 affords a considerable amount of sight. Those individuals who have some sight are referred to as "partially sighted." There are two types of partial sightedness: (1) those who can perceive objects and (2) those who can discriminate between daylight and darkness; this is known as "light perception." Those individuals with a complete lack of sight are referred to as "totally blind."

There are two classifications of total blindness: (1) those who have never seen, who are congenitally blind, and (2) those who have had some sight but have lost it, considered adventitiously blind.

Types of Deafness

The Committee on Nomenclature of the Conference of Executives of American Schools for the Deaf defines the deaf as those in whom the sense of hearing is nonfunctional for the ordinary purposes of life. This general group is made up of two distinct classes based entirely on the time of the hearing loss. They are (1) the congenitally deaf, or those who are born deaf, and (2) the adventitiously deaf, who were born with normal hearing but in whom the sense of hearing became nonfunctional later through illness or accident.

The hard of hearing are those individuals in whom the sense of hearing, although defective, is functional with or without a hearing aid.

Multihandicapped

Multihandicapped means concomitant impairments (such as mentally retarded-blind, mentally retarded-orthopedically impaired, etc.), the combination of which causes such severe educational problems that they cannot be accommodated in special education programs solely for one of the impairments. *The term does not include deaf-blind children.*

Deaf-Blind

Deaf-blind means concomitant hearing and visual impairments, the combination of which causes such severe communication and other developmental and educational problems that they cannot be accommodated in special education programs solely for deaf or blind children.

The term "deaf-blind" must not be taken literally. Deaf-blind children do have some residual vision and hearing. They may need the use of low vision aids and/or hearing aids to stimulate and produce functional vision and hearing in their early childhood years and subsequently throughout life.

In the realm of motor activity, the deaf-blind child with some functional vision has some advantages over the deaf-blind child who is totally blind, but each deaf-blind child should be exposed to all motor skills, depending upon his level of function. Motor skill development makes a contribution to the deaf-blind child's cognitive development. Whether the child is totally blind or not, every conceivable attempt should be made to develop his motor skills. Much can be learned about the visual and auditory capabilities of deaf-blind children through observation of their behavior, and they will offer information themselves, when they are able.

Mannerisms

Most deaf-blind children get little satisfaction from people or things around them. Their vision and hearing problems limit their physical activity and movement. Mannerisms consist of activities such as rocking, head banging, eye poking, light gazing, spinning and many other self-stimulating behaviors. These behaviors are bizarre, deviant and even destructive at times. Movement can help diminish these behaviors, if they are caused by frustration, emotional stress and boredom. It is far better to correct than punish a child when mannerisms occur.

Medical and Psychological Aspects

Medical and psychological aspects related to deaf-blindness must be considered. Reading the child's files and meeting with the school clinical, health and ancillary staff can be of much help and provide future direction for the deaf-blind child's motor program. Safety factors must be considered, and situations where severe bodily harm could result must be anticipated and guarded against.

Social Relationships and Peer Interaction

Social relationships and peer interaction must be encouraged. Depending on the level of function of the deaf-blind child, motor skills can serve as a bridge for social relationships and peer interaction in this part of the child's development.

Level of Functioning of Deaf-Blind Children

Low level functioning deaf-blind children are generally not toilet trained, do not imitate and are nonverbal. Borderline level functioning children are generally on the verge of being toilet trained, and can work with the teacher or their peers in many activities. High level functioning deaf-blind children are toilet trained, can imitate, and have some means of communication.

Transdisciplinary approach. One professional is designated as "primary therapist" with responsibilities for providing parent instruction and child programming in all developmental areas. Team members communicate across disciplines to share programming information needed by the primary therapist and to review progress.

Body image. Knowledge of the external body and its parts.

Self-concept. Inner knowledge of the body and how one feels about or sees oneself.

Motor skills. A particular type of body movement which is dependent on a certain degree of muscular control, which may be learned or improved through repetition of the movement.

CHAPTER THREE

EARLY MOVEMENT EXPERIENCES

I T IS OBVIOUS from the description of the characteristics of deaf-blind infants and young children in Chapter One that early home training is of prime importance, and that "parenting" must begin immediately with a deaf-blind child.

"Deaf-blind children can be helped, and more by their parents than any other person they will come in contact with in their childhood years," states the mother of a rubella deaf-blinded child (Freeman 1975).

EARLY HOME TRAINING IS CRUCIAL

If parents have prepared their child to work with other people, they will be off to a running start. If not, it will be necessary to start at the very lowest level of developmental activities, such as raising the head, sitting up and rolling from front to back.

It is important to be empathic with parents and realize the tremendous effort that has gone into working with their children from birth. An example of this is Matthew, an eight-year-old deaf-blind child, and his mother.

> At birth Matthew weighed one pound, fourteen ounces. He was prematurely born at seven months, the survivor of a twin birth, his brother Mark having died five days after birth. Matthew was hospitalized three months. He had heart surgery at eighteen days, when he weighed one pound, ten ounces. At three months he developed double hernias which were corrected by surgery.
>
> After he had been home one month, his mother realized that he was not following finger movements, and thus discovered, at four months, that Matthew could not see. He was totally blind.

13

He was having physical therapy and infant stimulation seven days a week. There was no startle reflex. His mother realized something was wrong, but did not know how to define it. She taught him to crawl and creep before he walked, which he did at 23 months independently, and was walking at 24 months. He started preschool at two years of age, in a class with five other handicapped children. He made no progress. There was no communication, and there were tantrums and behavior problems. His mother did not know where to turn for help.

At the age of four, he was given an *evoked response audiometry test.* There was absolutely no reaction to any kind of sound. It was at this time that his mother realized she had a deaf-blind child. Matthew was taken to another audiologist who elicited enough response to make him eligible for hearing aids. Since using hearing aids, the tantrums and negative behavior have almost disappeared. His mother had training in sign language for parents, and now communicates as well as possible with him.

The school situation remained unsatisfactory. Since he is a high functioning deaf-blind child, he did not fit in the multihandicapped unit, where most of the children were custodial and did not talk. Transportation was unsatisfactory as well, since he rode the school bus with the high school students who were undisciplined. She refused to put him in a deaf unit, which was advised by school authorities. She finally found a vision unit in an elementary school in another district, and established residence there so Matthew could attend the school. It was difficult for him to adjust to all the new activity and sound, to the point where he was almost transferred to a class for deaf children in another county. Some staff and "significant others" intervened, however, and since then he has made strides educationally.

His mother gives much credit for support to her family, especially her mother, and to her church, whose members helped with the therapies involved. The preschool teacher aided greatly with getting him to eat solid foods and with toilet training.

There have been many difficult times, but now, at eight years of age, Matthew can totally dress himself, bathes by himself and eats unassisted. He was totally toilet trained at seven. His mother uses "loves" and "pats" for rewards, but no foods.

His world is changing completely for the better, much to the credit of his teacher, who has been his continuous advocate. His mother has said that, "You'll never know how much it has taken to get him where he is, but the effort has been worth every minute."

As a help to other families who may wish to work with their deaf-blind children, a correspondence course for parents of deaf-blind children may be secured from The John Tracy Clinic (Thielman et al. 1973) which parents can follow, with guidance and encouragement at every step. It is a manual that deals not only with daily tasks, but with fine and gross motor movements as well.

Learning Steps (Southwest Regional Deaf-Blind Center 1976) is another helpful manual for teaching the very young deaf-blind child in a residential setting. It is also helpful for teaching motor skills in school situations.

ROLL - OVER

Figure 3-1. Manual sign for "Roll Over." Concepts after figures found in LEARN-ING STEPS (1976) pp 72, 73, 279, courtesy fo the California State Department of Education.

EARLY INTERVENTION IS A NECESSITY

The normal baby is aware of and curious about practically every-thing in the environment. The deaf-blind child shows no curiosity and requires nothing more as long as basic needs of bodily comforts are met. Without environmental movement experiences, the infant will remain in a state of mere sensation. Movement experiences, in the beginning, come from bodily movement by parent or teacher. Rocking in a chair and finger games are examples.

Stirring Incentive in Infancy

Some sort of incentive to move must be created, such as stimulating the child's interest in objects. This might be plaything that is liked, such as a lid or a box, something bright, shiny; a ball with a certain texture, something that squeaks, makes a noise or emits a puff of air when squeezed.

Reaching: A Milestone on the Road to Learning

When the child will reach for something (and this may take a long time) the way to learning is opened. Put the object or toy in different places—above, beside, behind—to increase body awareness. Inch it away so the child has to move toward it to possess it. Put it a little farther away; make it fun. The first time the child reaches for the toy that you offer, there is realization that there is an object outside of himself that can be possessed by effort on his part. Use signs and speak, for it is important that the child respond to signs or voice.

There Must Be a Reward System

Like any other person, the deaf-blind child blossoms when justifiably praised. The reward need not, and should not be a trinket or something to eat. Retrieving the toy can be its own reward, with you showing pleasure at this accomplishment. Devise a sign to show you are proud and happy that the child has done well. This can be a pat on the back—a sign for "well done." Say the words, "very good," as you give the child a pat on the back. Use that sign for the purpose only, and do not change it until the child has attained a higher level of communication. Signing is not that difficult; most signs are descriptive of what is to happen.

HAPPY

Figure 3-2. Manual sign for "Happy." Concepts after figures found in LEARNING STEPS (1976) pp 72, 73, 279, courtesy of the California State Department of Education.

Establishing Trust and Confidence

The child must develop awareness of his body. Confidence and trust must be established. To do this, the child must not only be aware of self, but must know that there is another person out there in whom trust and confidence can be placed. This is accomplished by being consistent, methodical and repetitive in your approach. Have a set routine; hopefully anticipation and expectation will stir within the child.

A Thing Becomes Meaningful When You Do Something With It

The first ideas a child has about things in the world are based on motor patterns. These arise as a result of handling *things*. Until the child picks up a ball and rolls or throws it, it is not different from an apple, which is also round. When the child eats the apple and rolls the ball they are different; each movement becomes a meaningful one. With all children, gesture precedes speech. So it is with the deaf-blind child, where we constantly look for a meaningful movement and not just a reflexive response. A motor program should be devised so that the child moves *toward* and *with* things. The child moves toward the toy to acquire it, and with the toy truck to make it go. Things should be made inviting, such as a box to be filled, a ball to be rolled.

Routine is Important

Play with the child at certain times, in a certain way, in a specific place. Make yourself the symbol of fun times; identify yourself as the person with whom the child can move and play, and, hopefully, run and jump and do stunts, later.

The foregoing paragraphs are optimistic ones. You will have some very bad moments, and perhaps complete failure some of the time. You may get kicked or bitten, or worse. Remember that your problems are minute compared to the child's, and if you move the child *one inch with meaning,* the child has *moved a mile* toward the world of reality.

CHAPTER FOUR

THE ROLE OF THE PHYSICAL EDUCATION TEACHER

Attitudes Toward the Deaf-Blind Staff

IN THE MAJORITY of deaf-blind programs, whether in residential schools for the blind or the deaf, or in institutions, or in day school programs, there may not be a full- or part-time physical education teacher to consult with the deaf-blind staff. When there is such a teacher, that person must make certain that attitudes are developed toward the deaf-blind staff that will contribute to the continuity and reinforcement of the deaf-blind child's total development.

Since the physical education teacher's background has been in motor activity, there may have been some exposure to the education of visually handicapped children or the education of deaf children, but the physical education teacher would certainly not have had a full program in the education of deaf-blind children such as other members of the teaching staff have had. It is thus incumbent upon the physical education teacher to learn everything possible regarding the characteristics of deaf-blind children through reading, observation and listening to those persons involved in the teaching process, and, particularly, to develop rapport with the deaf-blind staff. One of the first and major areas the deaf-blind staff can assist the physical education teacher with is that of communicating with the deaf-blind child at whatever functional level the child may be.

When scheduling the deaf-blind child for motor skills instruction, the deaf-blind staff should have maximum input. The physical education teacher and the classroom teachers should cooperate in determining when their children will attend motor skills and physical education classes. The classroom teacher may have from three to six children under her jurisdiction. They may be at similar or varied levels of cognitive or motor function. The teacher may wish to send a child to be with a group that is more similar in cognitive or motor function than his classmates. There are many cases where the motor ability of a low functioning deaf-blind child is higher than that of a high functioning deaf-blind child.

These deaf-blind children will be going through a variety of cognitive and motor programs during their school day. Their activities will include sorting, sequencing, co-active movement and language skills that are taught by the classroom teacher. She will know in which areas and when each particular child shows maximal attention, motivation and stimulation, and may have a preference of times she wishes to have specific children with her. On this basis a time slot will be set by the physical education teacher for her particular children to come for motor skills instruction.

Encourage Classroom Teachers to Observe Motor Skills

It should be emphasized that the physical education teacher should make classes open to the teachers of the deaf-blind children, as this promotes awareness, continuity and reinforcement on the part of both the classroom and physical education teachers. Though the classroom teacher may sometimes send a teacher aide, it is of great benefit for the teacher to come at frequent intervals so that she may become aware of the motor program in which her pupils are involved.

She can demonstrate the kind of communication she employs with her children and request the physical education teacher to employ the same, providing continuity in this area of development. Reinforcement becomes reciprocal when the classroom teacher explains her objectives for each child and the physical education teacher follows up. For example, if the teacher has the deaf-blind child learning the manual alphabet and the child is beginning to form and comprehend words in the classroom, the physical education teacher can begin finger spelling action words such as "run," "jump" and "hop" in the motor skills area and may request that the classroom teacher do the same with that particular child in the classroom. Reinforcement, both cognitive and motor, becomes the focal point in the child's learning experience. The children may learn to come to the motor skills room by themselves, as a lesson in orientation and mobility.

The transfer of training in motor skills to classroom activity can also be incorporated in the teacher's lesson plan. Communication among the members of a deaf-blind staff, of which the physical education teacher is a part, is extremely vital in accomplishing this.

Attitudes Toward the Deaf Blind Child

There is and there will always be a need for physical education people in special education as long as there are exceptional children who have cognitive and motor needs to be fulfilled. There is no end to the challenge that the deaf-blind child will present to the physical education graduate who has never worked with exceptional children, youth or adults. This child is a unique human being. His behavior is unique to his impairment, he is not just deaf-blind, he is multiply handicapped. The classroom teacher as well as the physical education teacher must be multiply-prepared to teach, train and motivate these deaf-blind children.

The physical education teacher must realize that the deaf-blind child has the basic needs of any "normal" child and should be given every opportunity to be exposed to experiences normal children are exposed to, with necessary modifications, adaptations and adjustments that will bring the deaf-blind child as close to normal behavior as possible.

With his various bizarre, deviant and autistic-like behaviors, the deaf-blind child presents the physical education teacher with a multitude of challenges. The deaf-blind child can make you laugh, or make you sad. He can be emotionally upsetting and frustrating. Nevertheless, the major concern is still the attitude the physical education teacher has toward these deaf-blind children. This attitude will dictate the philosophy and policy used in setting up their motor skills program.

Individual Versus Group Instruction

Although many deaf-blind children exhibit similar behaviors, they each also exhibit individual differences that are unique to each personality. The physical education teacher must be perceptive enough to pick up these individual differences and respond to them accordingly. This will take some time; it will, however, put the physical education teacher in a position where the behavior of the young deaf-blind children being taught can be predicted, channeled and controlled to a higher degree. This is very important, especially when working with several children at one time. It reflects the educational emphasis placed on individualized instruction within groups of children being taught. Individualized instruction in this case does not signify one-to-one instruction. It advocates the necessity to continue working with deaf-blind children in groups while simultaneously dealing with individual differences presented by each child in the group. When this is done properly, there is a smooth transition from one area of activity to another, and the focal points of that day's lesson are covered.

In extreme cases, it is necessary for the physical education teacher to take a single child for instruction, with the idea of integrating the child into a group, when that child is ready for group participation in the program.

Some high functioning deaf-blind children show very high cognition and motor performance as compared to low functioning children. The physical education teacher must not be caught up in the trap of showing bias toward the higher functioning child; there must be concern for the total development of all deaf-blind children, regardless of their motor performance or motor ability. The teacher must strive daily to bring deaf-blind children of low motor ability into closer proximity with those who have a higher level of motor ability. The teacher must also provide new motoric experiences for those children with existing high motor ability so that they will be challenged to put their acquired motor skills into even more complex problem-solving situations.

Encourage Peer and Social Interaction

The promotion of peer interaction and social development through motor skills should be an important concern of the physical education teacher. Because of a lack of social development and perhaps because of individual differences, peer interaction is practically nonexistent among deaf-blind children. Simply because children are in a group does not mean that they are all moving at the same time and moving together. High functioning deaf-blind children tend to be more receptive to interaction and social kinds of experiences than low functioning deaf-blind children. Motor activities that involve working with another child can be introduced to help low functioning deaf-blind children improve social and peer interaction and cooperation. Lead-up games and activities also help the low functioning child improve in this respect. When, and only when, deaf-blind children are ready for games of socialization that require cooperation, and understand the aspect of competition, should higher type motor skill activities be presented.

The Teacher Must Sell the Program

Ultimately, the physical education teacher must promote his own program. With all the technical aspects of devising the motor skills program and the theory behind it, how practical is it? Who makes it go? What makes it go, and how? The answer is the physical education teacher! Let us hope it will be the deaf-blind children involved in the programs to whom the physical education teacher really sells the program.

It is in this respect that the teacher's attitude toward the deaf-blind child is of utmost significance. He must employ "role-playing" to promote his program. His attitude toward role-playing can make or break the real enthusiasm that should be in a program of movement and play activities that will also enhance and contribute to the deaf-blind child's cognitive development.

Nonhandicapped children at this primary age level have a high play urge. With deaf-blind children, it usually has to be brought out with the help of an adult. The physical education teacher is in a position to take advantage of this. In order to bring out the element of play in these children, the physical education teacher must discard the "adult attitude" usually assumed and come down to the level of these deaf-blind children. Let them "see" him or her in this role, as the role-playing becomes a part of the personality of the physical education teacher.

At this point the physical education teacher becomes the "fun skills specialist," and rapport between the teacher and the deaf-blind child begins to develop. This produces the kind of interpersonal relationships that these children should experience. Furthermore, *any fears, frustrations or anxieties the physical education teacher may have should begin to disappear.* Deaf-blind children are children; they will not break when touched; they can respond. You can begin to enter their world—their environment—and you can invite them into a world and an environment of movement—movement which will help them in many, many ways.

Some of these children will undoubtedly be on various kinds of behavior modification programs as set up by their classroom teachers, but movement in a motor skills program that promotes structure with flexibility cannot be dismissed as a behavior modification program in itself.

Additional emphasis is placed here in that the physical education teacher must see all of the deaf-blind children in the program. When there are staffings on particular children, the input from the physical education teacher should be requested and encouraged. This reflects the awareness, continuity and reinforcement vital to the deaf-blind staff and gives the deaf-blind child the benefit of having a total diagnosis.

Personal Requisites of the Motor Skills Teacher

High Skill Level

The physical education teacher must be able to perform skillfully the activities which the children are taught, and be capable of demonstrating a high quality of movement when performing them. Analyzing movement with accuracy and judgement helps in assessing and evaluating the children in the program. The physical education teacher must also be creative and use imagination, especially with children who are at different levels of motor and cognitive development. The teacher must go beyond the concept of being a "regular" physical education teacher and consider himself or herself an adapted physical education specialist working with children who are multihandicapped.

Know Child's Biological Age

The physical education teacher must be aware of the biological as well as the chronological ages of the children. Biological age refers to the physical development of the neuromuscular system of the human organism. Deaf-blind children come in all sizes and shapes, some being under-developed and some over-developed for their chronological age. Knowing the child's biological age can help determine how much physical activity can be tolerated, as well as indicating readiness on the part of the child, developmentally. This knowledge also safeguards against injury to the child.

Good Health Is Necessary

The health of the teacher of deaf-blind children is very important. If the children are to benefit from instruction, the teacher must maintain the peak of health and fitness. Because of the nature of the deaf-blind children's problems, and because they are quite susceptible to upper respiratory infections and viruses, teachers and others working with them are vulnerable to contracting these communicable diseases. Physical education teachers have a lot of physical contact with the children and can also observe any abnormal behavior beyond routine conduct which might signify the child is ill, and not "just being uncooperative."

Stamina Is Important

Stamina is a part of being fit and healthy, and the physical education teacher must have much of it. Some deaf-blind children are very passive and others are extremely active. Whichever characteristic they possess or exhibit, they can be very exhausting to work with. If the physical education teacher does not already have it, it will be necessary to develop the stamina to keep up, pick up and catch up with these children.

Many of the activities in the motor skills program require mutual movement between the deaf-blind child and the teacher. This means there is some lifting, positioning and tactile involvement on the part of the physical education teacher. Most deaf-blind children need physical positioning to stimulate movement in certain activities, and it is absolutely necessary for the physical education teacher and the classroom teacher as well, to develop the stamina required to teach these movement activities.

Psychological and Emotional Stability

Psychological health and emotional stability must also be considered. They are as important as the teacher's physical health. There may be a personal need fulfillment on the part of the teacher in working with deaf-blind children. Hopefully this need fulfillment will not be greater than the need fulfillment of the children themselves. Otherwise, "burn-out" or "rust-out" can develop, causing teacher performance to decline. It is of great importance and significance to put the deaf-blind child and his needs before those of the teacher, when and wherever the deaf-blind child is taught.

High Tolerance Level

It is not always easy to cope with the multitude of problems deaf-blind children have. The length of time it takes for some children to acquire and retain certain basic skills can be frustrating to the physical education teacher. Many of these children are not toilet trained and may have accidents while in motor skills class. The swimming pool may become a big "potty" for some deaf-blind children. It is necessary to deal with these problems, and the physical education teacher must assume an important part in this phase of the child's development.

The physical education teacher will have to deal with tantrum behavior that deaf-blind children often have. Knowing why the tantrum occurred and what to do to bring the child out of it may take some considerable amount brainstorming. Along these same lines, some deaf-blind children exhibit self-abusing and self-mutilating behavior. There are many other self-stimulatory behaviors deaf-blind children exhibit which deter their attention span, making it difficult for the teacher to instruct them.

All in all, stamina and good health are vital to the teacher of deaf-blind children, and the physical education teacher must have a high threshold of psychological security and emotional stability to cope with the many problems deaf-blind children present.

CHAPTER FIVE

DEVELOPMENTAL THEORIES RELATED TO EDUCATIONAL APPROACHES

THERE ARE SEVERAL theoretical models that have relevance to the field of deaf-blind education. The Piagetian model is concerned with the way a child acts upon his environment, receives feedback and internalizes these experiences. Piaget, (1955) however, based his ideas on normal child development. There is no accounting for the effects that a double sense deficit might have on a child's interaction, or lack of it, with the environment. The deaf-blind infant, as we have seen, does little more with the environment than exist within it; interactions with his surroundings must be guided and prompted by others. Most deaf-blind children fall into Piaget's (1955) first stage of development, the sensorimotor level. Advantage may be taken in application of teaching techniques at this level. For this reason, work with deaf-blind children should begin as soon after birth as possible (van Dijk 1965).

Behavior analysis and modification is another approach to teaching deaf-blind children. Many problems are encountered with this approach also, as many deaf blind children are tactually defensive, and will have no part of physical reinforcement. Many of them also do not like a great variety of foods. With touch and taste approaches limited, and even less potential for stimulation through sight and hearing, this method presents challenges. It is used, however, with many of these children, and the physical educator should be aware of any behavior modification plans being used with a child so that he can be consistent with the behavior plan the teacher and all others are using. The point is that physical education should not be used as an instrument for correcting negative or inappropriate behaviors, but rather to increase motor skills for the deaf-blind child.

27

MYKLEBUST'S HIERARCHIES OF EXPERIENCE

Deaf-blind children are classified according to three functional levels of performance: low, borderline and high, which are significantly related to their communication capabilities. These, in turn, are related to their attainment of certain levels of experience, and thus, a third educational approach concerns language development.

Myklebust (1964) states, in his studies of language development in the deaf, that *experience constitutes the basis of all behavior*, including language behavior, and that language is the means whereby experience is symbolized and communicated. He views experience in terms of levels or hierarchies, and compares the experience of the deaf with that of normally hearing individuals.

The Hierarchies of Experience are categorized into the levels of Sensation, Perception, Imagery, Symbolization, and Conceptualization, as experience moves from concreteness to abstraction.

In the nonverbal child the lack of language very deeply influences behavior. The deaf-blind child is five or six, or even older, before grasping the idea of symbols (Magin 1980). Thus the hierarchical frame of reference is useful to indicate a third educational approach that may be taken with deaf-blind children at the three functional levels of performance, as they move from the level of sensation to perception, imagery, symbolization and conceptualization.

The fourth model often used by teachers and workers with the deaf-blind is that of van Dijk, whose theories have arisen from his work with deaf-blind children at St. Michielsgestal in the Netherlands. Dr. van Dijk's theories have been misinterpreted by some people, possibly through translation, and they are controversial in some instances.

When speaking of deaf-blind children Dr. van Dijk states that their world goes no further than their own body. It is the goal of education to enlarge this world, that is, to humanize this child. This education must encourage a *distance* between Me — the Ego — and Things. The van Dijk model begins with the teaching of body knowledge and motor development.

Myklebust's Hierarchies
of Experience

Functional Levels
of Performance
of Deaf-Blind
Children

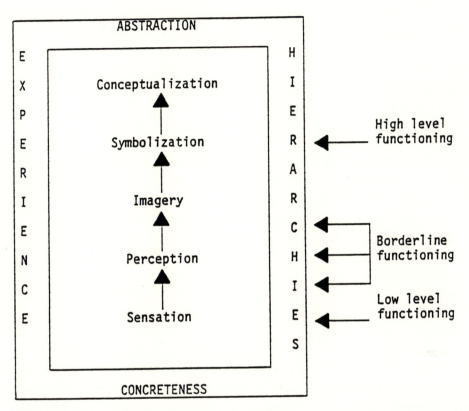

Diagram 5-I. A schematic presentation of Myklebust's Hierarchies of Experience* and the Functional Levels of Performance of Deaf-Blind Children, showing where remedial training must be focused.

*Courtesy H. Myklebust, *Psychology of Deafness, Sensory Deprivation, Learning and Adjustment*, 2nd ed., p. 225, Grune and Stratton, Inc., Orlando. (1964).

van Dijk's Co-active Movement Model

The early stage of moving and acting together with the child is referred to in the van Dijk model as *co-active movement*. In developing the body image, the child and teacher move and act together to provide experiences. In the beginning the child does not discriminate between the environment and his body. This is no awareness of another person—no personal relationship. The child is moved through different motor patterns, guided by the teacher. The teacher or parent moves the child's arms, legs and body through various movements, such as rolling over, kicking or reaching.

Gradually, distance is *increased* between the teacher and child, that is, the child experiences tactually movements made by the teacher, exploring in turn the teacher's movements, by touch. As an example, the teacher's arms are raised overhead, while the child follows the movement by touching the moving arms. The child's arms are then raised along with the teacher's, as they perform the movement together. A time factor is then added, as the pupil and the teacher *take turns*. The teacher initiates the movement, then the child makes the same motion. The child is now *imitating* the teacher's movement.

There are two stages in imitation: *mirroring* and *paralleling*. Mirroring implies that the child is aware of being opposite and very separate from the teacher, whose role shifts from stimulator to that of a model. Symmetrical exercises such as clapping hands, kneeling and carrying a ball are used. Asymmetrical exercises should also be used, such as lifting one arm, then the other, and touching specific body parts, first with one hand, then the other.

Parallel activities bring out more independent action, providing more *distance-sense* acquisition. These activities stimulate both fine and gross motor coordination. They begin with simple imitation. An example of this is the "scoot," which provides a good base of support for balance and coordination. The child and teacher sit side by side and scoot along the floor mat, together. The teacher still serves as a model, but the child uses the model as a reference, gaining more independence. More complex locomotor activities are then added, such as knee walking, jumping and hopping.

There may never be a concise philosophy of education for deaf-blind students, but the importance of the involvement of the sensory modalities in the learning process cannot be overestimated. Van Dijk indicates that the development of the senses is very complicated—the senses do not develop singly, and if one part in the sensory development is not functioning, there is complete disorder (Walsh, in Walsh and Holzberg 1981).

With this in mind, the intrasensory processes are now reviewed as they affect the body image and perceptual-motor development.

Figure 5-1. Coactive movement: Mirroring.

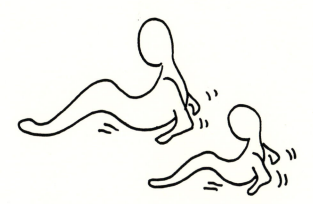

Figure 5-2. Coactive movement: Paralleling.

PERCEPTUAL-MOTOR DEVELOPMENT IN DEAF-BLIND CHILDREN

In order for perceptual-motor development to occur, there must be some kind of sensory stimulation with some sort of motor action as a result. The types of stimulation referred to are visual, auditory and tactile.

The Intra-Sensory Process

In normal child development, all the sense modalities interact with each other: the vestibular system (balance) with vision; vision with audition; vision with taction and audition with the tactile modality. In the case of the deaf-blind child, with severe impairments of vision and hearing, feedback from the senses will be altered and they will be behind or latent in development. Many deaf-blind children begin to show some sort of "catch up" phenomenon when they can imitate movement and interpret auditory stimuli. If there is a sensory deficit, there will be some motor and cognitive retardation. If the child has a deficit in motor development, sensory and cognitive development will be affected. The lack of love and basic security may retard or alter sensory, motor or cognitive development.

Development of the body image is affected by the intrasensory process. The body image of children can be considered as developing through three stages or levels (Bladergroen n.d.).

Level I is the pre-reflexive level—the unconscious state of the body image.

Level II is the sensory-motoric level—the experience of the body has a quality of totality.

Level III is the level of the development of the body image—the awareness of the other person, who can be seen, felt and heard.

At the second level, if a system is dysfunctioning or lacking, as it is with deaf-blind children, there will be disturbances in the process of differentiation. In the case of the deaf-blind child who has some vision, strive to increase this potential; if the child has some hearing, stress this potential, in the hope of minimizng such disturbances. If there is a severe deficit in both hearing and vision, tactile stimulation is employed (Myklebust 1964).

Classic Theories of Perceptual-Motor Development

In many ways the earlier theories of perceptual-motor development have provided no appreciable evidence of improvement in intellectual capacities for subjects exposed to their methods. In many other ways they have been significant in bringing to the forefront the necessity for motor experiences to improve cognition as it relates to the various systems of communication. Four pioneer theories are reviewed briefly here, with the several individuals responsible for their development.

1. *The Theory of Cortical Integration* — Carl H. Delacato.
   Movement activities at various developmental levels will somehow improve the functioning of various parts of the central nervous system which in turn will positively influence other peripheral processes (vision, audition, etc.), purportedly mediated by the same portions of the brain which control the motor functions practiced.

2. *The Theory of Perceptual Training Through Movement* — Newell C. Kephart; G. W. Getman; and Ray H. Barsh.
   All learning stems from motor functioning, which contributes to perceptual development, which in turn forms the basis of intelligence.

3. *The Dynamic Theory* — James N. Oliver.
   Improvement is academic and intellectual processses will occur indirectly, as motivation and success in play are realized by children, which in turn heightens self-concept and a willingness to try harder at academic as well as motor tasks.

4. *The Central Cognitive Theory* — Bryant J. Cratty, James Humphery; G. Lawrence Rarick; and Geoffrey Broadhead.
   Movement activities which provoke thought may improve intelligence. Research findings suggest that retarded children be taught to think more efficiently through movement, by being encouraged to think about the movement activities in which they engage.

These earlier theories, the foundation of current perceptual-motor theories, focused on the enhancement of voluntary movement. Ayres (1972) believes that motor training should be directed toward the subcortical levels of the brain, and has exerted a powerful influence in switching the basis of adapted physical education teaching from perceptual-motor to the sensory integration theory.

Williams (1983) differentiated between intrasensory and intersensory integration, whereas Ayres (1972) views sensory integration as a global concept (Sherrill 1986). One might conjecture that Williams (1983), in her belief that two or three systems (tactile-kinesthetic-visual) are intra-dependent and considered as one for the purpose of improving reading and writing skills, is not too far removed from van Dijk (1965) in his belief that the senses do not develop singly, so that one (or more) nonfunctioning mode(s) create(s) complete disorder. Williams (1983) defines intersensory integration as the ability to use several sources of sensory integration simultaneously to help in adapting to the environment and problem solving. She defines three levels of intersensory functioning; a low-level automatic mode of integration, which is inborn and manifested by reflex integration and sound postural reactions; a higher order of integration that primarily involves cognitive discrimination of shapes, colors, sizes and sounds; and a cognitive/conceptual level of integration which involves transfer of ideas or concepts across different sense modalities. The impact of this presents a formidable barrier for children with a double sensory deficit.

In summary, perceptual-motor skills development has been suggested as being benefit when functions of the nervous system are defective and, through body movement, is of benefit as the most direct means of enhancing body image and self-concept. In general, motor skills development improves behavior in deaf-blind children through control of movement. All behavior has a motor aspect.

CHAPTER SIX

MOTOR SKILLS DEVELOPMENT OF DEAF-BLIND AND VISUALLY IMPAIRED CHILDREN

A REVIEW OF MOTOR DEVELOPMENT

IT IS IMPERATIVE that we look at the terms used in the various related areas of motor development. What, exactly, is motor development?

Defining Motor Development Terms

Motor Development

Motor development includes the growth and elaboration of the muscular and nervous systems of an individual. It is a continuous process which is affected by many factors, two of the major ones being maturation and experience.

Maturation. Involves orderly changes in development, based on a necessary aging or temporal element.

Experience. Denotes all environmental interactions, including specific movement training, that an individual may encounter.

Perceptual-motor Development

Perceptual-motor development incorporates the processes of organizing the environmental stimuli, or sensory input, processing them on the basis of past experiences and present circumstances, and reacting in a way that is meaningful to the individual, or motor output.

Gross Motor Development

Gross motor development involves the employment of the large mus-

groups and generally includes the whole body. Activities such as kicking, pushing, carrying objects and throwing are examples.

Fine Motor Development

Fine motor development tasks are generally confined to the small muscles of the extremities. These are often manipulative movements which are related to the development of eye-hand coordination. Cutting with scissors, stringing beads or threading a needle are examples.

Locomotor Development

Locomotor development pertains to patterns or skills whereby the individual moves or propels himself through space. These include rolling, creeping (hands and knees), crawling (on stomach), walking, running, jumping and related movements.

Motor Skills Development

Motor skills development includes a particular type of body movement which is dependent on a certain degree of muscular control, which may be learned or improved through physical repetition. Hopefully, the individual should develop a motor pattern.

Motor pattern. Refers to the movement characteristics in the performance of a physical skill. For example, in reviewing the development of the fundamental skill of walking, an individual begins with hesitant "toddling" steps with the feet wide apart, foot placement on full soles of the feet and arms extended outward sideways for balance. There is a gradual transition to a mature pattern of the full leg swing, heel-toe weight transfer, and oppositional cross-lateral arm swing.

Motor Components

There are seven basic movement qualities, or motor components. The extent to which they are developed determines an individual's general motor ability. The seven basic components are: agility, balance, coordination, endurance, flexibility, speed and strength.

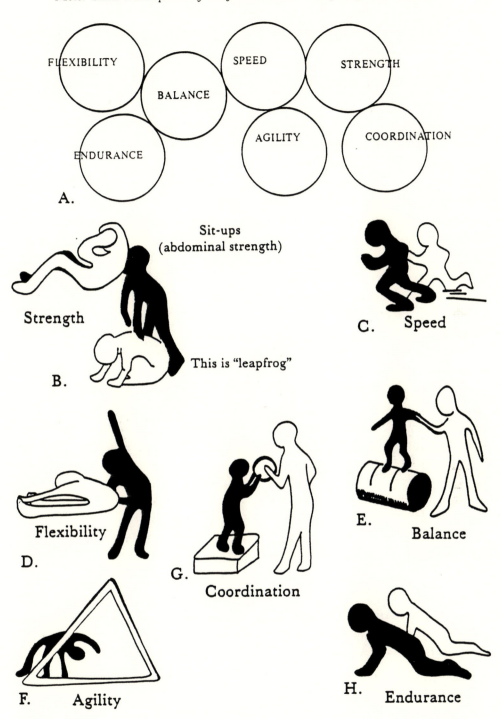

Figure 6-1. The seven basic components of Motor Activity: (A) The seven components relate to each other; (B) Strength; (C) Speed; (D) Flexibility; (E) Balance; (F) Agility; (G) Coordination; (H) Endurance.

MOTOR PROBLEMS OF THE DEAF-BLIND

Some of the problems of the deaf-blind and what can be done to diminish them are considered here. The preschool blind child is also included in this category, as this program could be implemented to diminish similar problems in this unique group.

Motor problems of the deaf-blind are not a simple combination of the problems of the deaf and the problems of the blind. Every deaf-blind child presents a different group of motor problems. Because of the complex nature of these, a single program to fit the motor needs of a class of deaf-blind children generally will not be effective. There are, however, certain problems common to many deaf-blind children in the motor area which can be targeted by several members of the professional staff. The formulation of the following objectives is an example of the physical education teacher cooperating with the physical therapist is working with the children. Examples of corrective activities have been added as illustrations of remedial activity.

GENERAL OBJECTIVES FOR MOTOR PROGRAMS

Motor programs for the deaf-blind should include the following general objectives.

Prevent Superimposed Deformities

This means that movement patterns are introduced that will "break up" the fetal or twisted positions into which these children lapse. The log roll, in which the child rolls full length, with arms extended overhead, along a mat, is an example of corrective activity.

Reduce Random Stereotype Movement

Movement such as flicking and fanning the fingers and hands and rocking back and forth are examples of this objectionable type movement. Introducing a meaningful task will help divert these mannerisms.

Decrease Abnormal Body Patterns

The children get their bodies into abnormal shapes which are self-stimulating, such as twisting the arms and legs around each other, like "noodles." Introduce gross body movement such as arm swings, kicking and stretching.

Increase the Capacity to Perform Functional Activities

These include walking, sitting, grasping objects and eating techniques. Fundamental motor skills apply universally to these activities.

Utilize Auditory and Visual Cues

Where there is the slightest potential for enhancing hearing or vision, every effort should be made to do so. Assess the potential; use colors, ring bells, use sounds rather than always hands-on or body movement activities.

Increase Sensory-motor Processing

Develop cutaneous, proprioceptive and kinesthetic capacities. Touch the child in the same location when guiding a task, get the child in the same position for an activity and use the same command, consistently and without variation.

Motor programs for deaf-blind children are unsuccessful because (1) they fail to set appropriate expectations for function by the child, and (2) there is inconsistency in implementing the motor skills intervention program. Success for the program is much more predictable if some general rules for facilitating motor function of deaf-blind children are observed.

General Rules for Facilitating Motor Function

Intensive and Frequent Motor Stimulation

Intensive and frequent motor stimulation is needed for the deaf-blind child to reach normal developmental milestones. Short, intensive and repetitive instructional periods are required. When taking turns, have a very short period of activity in a simple movement, then a rest, then the movement again, such as jumping over an object.

Perform Motor Activities as Slowly as Possible

There should be no racing to the finish. Competition comes when the deaf-blind child has been prepared for such activity.

Positioning and Propping Are Important

The child may have to be moved into position and propped or held there, in order to develop the capacity to assume a position independently. Pillows can be used as props to assist a child to learn to sit up.

Coactive Help Is Needed

In order for the child to learn to scoot, go along side, doing the same scooting movement.

Small Increments Are Needed

Small increments in motor activity are needed rather than totally new motor experiences. Before teaching a child to jump rope, teach jumping, then jumping over a stationary rope on the floor.

Mastery of Skills Takes a Longer Period of Time

A longer period of time is required for deaf-blind than for non-handicapped children to effectively master a task. Do not assume a skill once taught is once learned. Review skills, over and over.

Help Associate Activity With a Goal

Help is required in associating a movement with a goal. Set a goal for a task: three hops in a row, or the length of the mat.

Talk to and Signal to the Children

These children should be talked to and signalled to, in keeping with the highest potential utilization of any sight or hearing present. Repeat instructions and wait for responses. Use colors and noisemakers.

Locomotion in the Upright Walking Position

The most crucial period in gross motor development is the beginning of locomotion in the upright walking position. In order to facilitate the development of this function, the child should never be left standing alone without support from you or a stable object. Clear all obstacles out of the way. Both the child's arms are extended in front of the body, fingertips on yours. Remove yours and have the child move toward you. If the child is capable of walking independently but lacks confidence, the following suggestions may help.

1. Walk behind the child with two fingers under each arm at the shoulder. Lessen your support and slowly release your fingers until the child walks alone.
2. Attach a rope to two stable objects about as high as the child's waist to use as a guide for balance.
3. Hold a piece of broom handle or yardstick about twelve or fifteen

inches long at one end and have the child hold the other end. Walk with the child. When you feel the child gaining confidence, gradually lessen your support. Do not release your hold too soon, as the child will not hold the stick the next time.

4. Tie a string to a favorite plaything. The child holds the toy and you hold the string. Pull the string so the child must move to keep possession of the toy. Gradually slacken the string until the child is walking, then release the string.

A good rule. Daily practice is compulsory. Until a child walks, few new activities can be initiated.

MOTOR PERFORMANCE OBJECTIVES

When planning a motor skills program for deaf-blind children, there are some long-term, broad, on-going goals for which the instructor must make provision.

Long-Term, On-going Goals

1. Introduce to each child a new environment for exploratory movement.
2. Help each child improve kinesthetic awareness.
3. Teach each child new physical skills.
4. Help each child develop improved body image and self-concept.
5. Help the child TO HAVE FUN.

There must be specific assessment procedures and instructional purposes or goals to facilitate the motor skills program.

Assessment and Programming for Motor Skills Instruction

Assess the present level of each deaf-blind child in the following areas: (1) motor skill development and motor readiness, (2) locomotor and nonlocomotor skill development, (3) body image and self-concept, (4) hearing and vision (employ materials and equipment in keeping with the child's potential), (5) eye-hand and eye-foot coordination.

Retain growth charts and take height and weight measures twice yearly.

Promote the social interaction for each child through group motor skill activities.

Plan activities and experiences that are conducive to the transfer of training of motor skills acquired and retained.

Make specific recommendations and require motor skills development for each child.

Instruct staff and family members in methods of teaching, stimulating and motivating further motor skills development for each child.

The Individual Motor Program[1]

Since each deaf-blind child's needs are different from others, and in order to achieve the goals, objectives and purposes that have been stated, an individual motor program must be devised for each child. To increase motor function in deaf-blind children, first recognize the problems and then focus on the major difficulty.

The following steps are recommended for improving motor function in the deaf-blind child:

1. Recognize the problem (Evaluate).
2. Focus on the major difficulty (Select).
3. Investigate the nature and extent of this difficulty (Evaluate in depth).
4. Develop an intervention program with help from parents and professionals (Plan).
5. Implement the intervention program in the classroom and living environment (Teach).
6. Evaluate the nature and rate of change (Reevaluate).
7. Revise the intervention (Replan).

SPECIAL METHODS OF INSTRUCTION AND EVALUATION

With such severe sensory deprivation, deaf-blind children are classified according to levels of function rather than chronological age or traditional intelligence tests. The three levels of function are low functioning, borderline functioning and high level functioning children.

---

[1]Service and Delivery: The School, the Parents and the Individual Education Program (IEP), see Chapter Eight.

Adapting Levels of Teaching to Functional Levels

When the motor skills program is devised, the physical education teacher, after meeting with the deaf-blind staff, and having read the files on each child, must gear the level of teaching to the level of function of each child in the program.

Low level functioning children do not imitate and are nonverbal; borderline children can work with the teacher or their peers in many activities, and high level functioning children can imitate and have some means of communication.

The communication level of each child is of significance. Some deaf-blind children may be nonverbal and others may be preverbal. There may be some deaf-blind children who are verbal and others who are using signing and finger spelling. There may be some who have expressive language skills and others who have receptive language skills. All of these factors are of great concern to the classroom teacher and to the physical education teacher. It is also necessary to know where these children are cognitively, as well as motorically, in order to get responses from them.

Adapting the level of teaching to the level of function facilitates the amount of material that can be taught within a certain timetable. If there are children with functional vision, the motor skills teacher demonstrates the motor skills activity for those particular children. They must be at the level of imitation and have a high attention span to benefit from this method. If the children are not at the level of imitation, the methodology employed is entirely different. The teacher explores the approach to which the child is most receptive, no matter how primitive it may be, beginning at the lowest level of experience, sensation, and working upward through the hierarchical categories of Myklebust, perhaps to the highest level, conceptualization.

For those children with some functional vision, flash cards can be used effectively in the motor skills class.

THE SIX-POINT FIGURE FLASH CARDS

Flash cards have been used for many years in elementary classrooms for teaching many subjects where a visual image facilitates the learning process. In keeping with the idea of using whatever amount of vision a deaf-blind child might have, flash cards also serve a useful purpose in the motor activity class.

The figures are six-point outline drawings of bodies, on 8½" x 11" stiff cards, representing a figure performing a motor skill. The figure has a head, a body, two arms and two legs (thus the six points). The head and body are basically curved, and the arms and legs are straight or at an angle, depending on the activity drawn. The cards can be laminated on flexible cardboard so they will tolerate wear and tear and handling by the children when held up close to their eyes.

The flash cards are used primarily for the pregymnastic skills of rolling, scooting, creeping, crawling, monkey walk, crab walk, walking on knees and forward and backward rolls. The children can look closely at the flash cards and then perform the activities, also saying the name of the stunt, in some cases. The cards can be used both in the motor activity room and the classroom, transferring training between the classroom teacher and the specialist in motor activity. The flash cards can also be used as an independent activity.

High functioning pupils who have enough vision to see the figures and whose cognition is improving can also draw these six-point figures when requested to do so. Sketching the figures enhances the child's concept of self and body image. This task becomes a high level activity as the child combines the motor activity performance with the sketch.

Teach in Any Area Available

Do not let limited space prevent the giving of maximum effort.

Activities in the motor skills program can be taught in any area available, at home as well as at school. A list of areas that have been utilized for the activities includes:

An indoor playroom	A small bedroom
Teacher's classrooms	A large basement
The swimming pool	The gymnasium (or
Hallways	part of it)

Scheduling and Planning Classes[2]

Aquatic activities are once a week in the pool. This is a one-on-one activity, facilitated with the help of volunteer instructors. The section on aquatics in Chapter Seven describes this in more detail. A routine for instruction, with further details will be found there.

---

[2]IEP, see Chapter Eight.

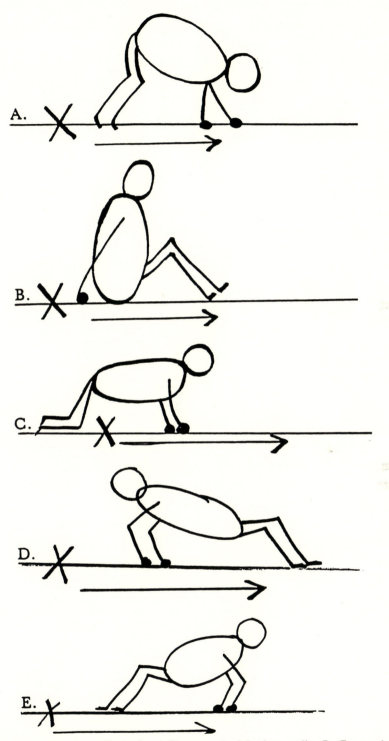

Illustration 6-1. Six-point Flash Card Figures: A. Monkey walk; B. Forward scoot; C. Creeping; D. Crabwalk forward; E. Crabwalk backwards.

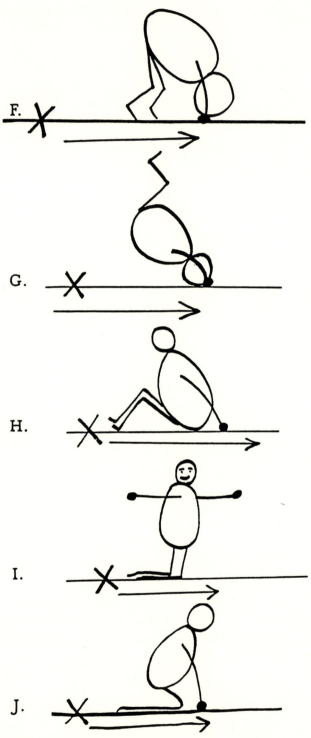

Illustration 6-2. Six-point Flash Card Figures: F. Forward roll; G. Backwards roll; H. Scoot backwards; I. Knee walk; J. Knee scoot.

Illustration 6-3. Sketches drawn by David, age 8, high functioning deaf-blind child: A. "Forward roll"; B. "Angel balance."

A.

B.

Illustration 6-4. Sketches drawn by Carolyn, age 8, high functioning deaf-blind child: A. "Knee walk"; B. "Creeping."

Motor skills classes are for thirty minutes daily with no less than two or more than four children in a group.

Nonambulatory children come alone for fifteen minutes.

Creativity, imagination or variations cannot possibly be written into this program; these factors must be provided by the individual teachers.

UNIT ACTIVITY INSTRUCTIONAL SCHEDULE[3]

The following is an example of an instructional schedule. It is beneficial for parents and teachers to be aware of this schedule, so that reinforcement can be given at home, at school and in the classroom. It keeps the teacher organized and goal-oriented.

CHILDREN FUNCTIONING AT LOW LEVEL

September October November December	January February March	April	May
Balance and Coordination Activities	Pre-gymnastic Skills and Stunts	Ball Skills	Review All Units
Locomotor Skills (First Four)	Doorway Chinning Bar Activities	Trapeze Skills (2nd time)	Assess Progress
Trapeze Skills			

CHILDREN FUNCTIONING AT BORDERLINE AND HIGH LEVELS

September	October	November December	January February March	April	May
Locomotor Skills (All Eight)	Balance and Coordination Activities	Ball Skills	Pre-gymnastic Skills and Stunts	Locomotor Skills (2nd time)	Review All Units
			Trapeze Skills	Ball Skills (2nd time)	Assess Progress
			Doorway Chinning Bar Exercises		

[3]IEP, see Chapter Eight.

EVALUATION TECHNIQUES

Too often educators test only because that is what they are expected to do. Somehow, the word "teacher" has become equated with "testing." The objectives of the system and the + , − , or A, E have no meaning unless the instructor has tested to discover how well students have accomplished the objectives of the unit. Tests should be constructed immediately after the formulation of motor performance objectives. The motor performance objectives for the various units which are included in a motor skills program for the deaf-blind were outlined in the preceding pages. Following are some suggested evaluation techniques that have proven successful.

Evaluating the motor performance of deaf-blind children is an extremely difficult task. "Erratic" has to be the best one-word description of their progress. Many deaf-blind children are not easily motivated to improve. They pay no heed to the unwritten social law upon which much learning is based: the desire to please. Such a child may be able to do a forward roll, but if he does not want to do one when the motor skills specialist is testing him, no amount of coaxing will persuade him to perform his best.

Nonsocial reinforcers such as cookies, candy, cereal, etc. are often helpful in motivating students, but some deaf-blind children are tactile-defensive and will not respond to such rewards. A "good-bad" chart with stars might be more effective with the tactile-defensive child. Remember too, that it is best to move the child from *extrinsic* to more *intrinsic* types of rewards. Social praise is a rewarding experience for the deaf-blind child. Hopefully, he will discover that the activities alone are rewarding. We must teach these special children the joys of accomplishment.

Because of this motivation problem, the physical education teacher's evaluation should be a continuous one over the period of an entire unit. A daily log should be kept on each child. Task analysis charts are invaluable.

Besides being an excellent way of keeping a daily record of progress, task analysis charts break down complex motor skills into their component movements. This enables the motor skills specialist to note even small steps toward improvement. Because progress is usually quite slow when working with deaf-blind children, an instructor may become easily discouraged if he constantly focuses on the whole skill. Task analysis charts move the key focal point from overall performance to the small parts that make up each motor skill. Table 6-II illustrates how task analysis data may be tallied.

Table 6-I
TASK ANALYSIS CHART

Forward Roll	*Independently*	*Some Help*	*Much Help*
1. Gets into initial position.			
2. Tuck head.			
3. Pushes with hands.			
4. Pushes with feet.			
5. Rolls straight.			
6. Gets into position to repeat.			

Table 6-II
EXAMPLE OF TASK ANALYSIS TALLY SHEET

Date	*Number of skills done independently*	*Number of "some helps"*	*Number of "much helps"*	*Total number of skills*
1-15-74	18	10	6	34
1-16-74	22	6	6	34
1-17-74	26	5	3	34
1-18-74	22	6	6	34
1-19-74	23	2	9	34

Table 6-III
EXAMPLE OF SIMPLE GRID CHART

Activities	*Jim*	*Nancy*	*Tim*
1. Simon Says			
a. head	A	B	A
b. front	A	B-	B +
c. feet	B-	B	A
2. Obstacle Course	A, Very Good 52.0 sec.	C- 72.3 sec.	B + 59.1 sec.
3. Moves box in relationship to body planes.	B +	C	A, Great!
4. Pushes cart through weave pattern.	B-	C + Much Better!	A-

If task analysis is not feasible for a particular unit due to the activities included or lack of time, a simple grid may be constructed for daily notes. Such a grid may also serve as a daily lesson plan.

Table 6-IV

MOTOR SKILLS CHART

Name	Jumps independently	Jumps with assistance	Does not jump	Runs independently	Runs with assistance	Does not run	Hops independently	Hops with assistance	Dates
1. John									
2. Mary									
3. David									
4. Carol									
5. Ted									

Skill charts are also quite useful. Evaluation dates should be recorded in the right hand section and the check marks should be color coded to correspond with these testing dates.

Several different grading scales are employed quite effectively in work with deaf-blind children. One system is a simple three point scale:

+ = Can perform independently.
0 = Can perform with assistance.
− = Cannot perform at present.

Following is a more complex scale which requires the instructor to make more precise subjective judgments.

A = Performs independently most of the time.
B = Can perform independently but usually requires some prodding.
C = Can perform with some tactile assistance.
D = Can perform with much tactile assistance.
E = Cannot perform at present.
NA = Not applicable.

Grades may be recorded daily on a grid, thereby shortening note taking time.

Objective testing measures should be taken whenever possible. The time it takes the child to run through an obstacle course should be recorded. The number of times he can hop on one foot before touching down with the other foot should be counted and the distance he can long jump should be measured. All this data will enable the educator to evaluate motor performance more objectively and may lead towards the development of "norms" for deaf-blind and other multihandicapped children.

THREE-YEAR PROGRESS ASSESSMENT REPORT

In addition to skills scales, use an annual progress assessment, of a very simple design. Color coded charts or graphs and written progress reports are used, so that the motor skills teacher and the classroom teacher can look at the accomplishments the deaf-blind student has attained.

There is also a height and weight growth chart for each child:

INDIVIDUAL HEIGHT AND WEIGHT GROWTH CHART

Child's Name_____

Date of Birth_____

Assessment Date

Age _____   _____

Age _____   _____

Age _____   _____

Height _____   _____

Height _____   _____

Height _____   _____

Weight _____   _____

Weight _____   _____

Weight _____   _____

CHAPTER SEVEN

EVALUATION SCALES FOR
FUNDAMENTAL MOTOR SKILLS

The Motor Skill Scales are used for assessment in the areas of:

Locomotor Activities
Pregymnastic Activities
Balance and Coordination
Swinging Trapeze
Doorway Chinning Bar
Ball Handling
Aquatic Activities

Each scale is arranged in orderly sequence from the lesser to the greater degree of difficulty. There are no grading scales, or "good, fair or poor" performance levels. It takes a very extended length of time, sometimes several years, for a deaf-blind child to perform a motor skill at the "normal" level.

"Satisfaction," for each child, means accomplishment at the level of the next small step. These scales are therefore checklists rather than grading scales. To show progression, use the date of accomplishment rather than a check mark. Use a different color for each evaluation period, as: red marks for Fall, green marks for Spring.

LOCOMOTOR ACTIVITIES

The child should be able to perform at the lower skill level before proceeding to the next level, i.e., start with "walking," then "running," "jumping" and on up the scale to the "slide." Many low-functioning children will not be ambulatory to the point of walking upright. These children should go to Pregymnastics for log rolls (full body contact) and the four-point contact skills, such as creeping and the crab walk.

CHECKLIST

Lower   _____   Walks independently
Skill   _____   Walks with assistance
Level   _____   Does not walk
   _____   Runs independently
   _____   Runs with assistance
   _____   Does not run
   _____   Jumps independently
   _____   Jumps with assistance
   _____   Does not jump
   _____   Jumps from a height independently
   _____   Jumps from a height with assistance
   _____   Does not jump from a height
   _____   Jumps over an object independently
   _____   Jumps over an object with assistance
   _____   Does not jump over an object
   _____   Jumps rope independently
   _____   Jumps rope with assistance
   _____   Does not jump rope
   _____   Hops independently
   _____   Hops with assistance
   _____   Does not hop
   _____   Skips independently
   _____   Skips with assistance
   _____   Does not skip
   _____   Gallops independently
   _____   Gallops with assistance
   _____   Does not gallop
   _____   Leaps independently
   _____   Leaps with assistance
   _____   Does not leap
Higher   _____   Slides independently
Skill   _____   Slides with assistance
Level   _____   Does not slide

PREGYMNASTICS ACTIVITIES

Pregymnastic activities consist of the following: log rolls, scooting, creeping (hands and feet), crawling (on stomach), monkey walk (hands and feet), crab walk (hands and knees, back to floor), knee walk, duck walk, creeping with peer on back (horse-back), forward and backward rolls, headstands and cartwheels. Such activities call for soft landings, so mats or other soft areas are required. Observe that these activities progress from full body contact (and a low center of gravity) in the log roll, through four-point body contact, in creeping and crab walks, to two-point body contact in knee walking. The knee walk encourages lifting the knees, so that when walking upright, the knee bend is facilitated. The horse-back ride calls for interaction between two persons, stimulating awareness of each other.

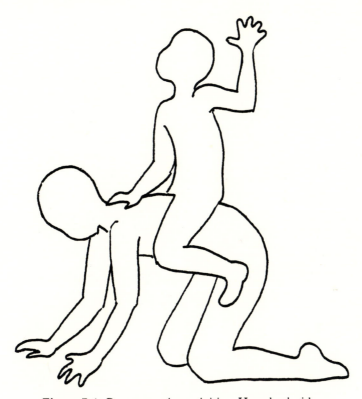

Figure 7-1. Pregymnastics activities: Horseback ride.

CHECKLIST

_____	Log rolls independently
_____	Log rolls with assistance
_____	Does not log roll
_____	Scoots forward independently
_____	Scoots forward with assistance
_____	Does not scoot forward
_____	Scoots backward independently

_____	Scoots backward with assistance
_____	Does not scoot backward
_____	Scoots on knees independently
_____	Scoots on knees with assistance
_____	Does not scoot on knees
_____	Creeps independently
_____	Creeps with assistance
_____	Does not creep
_____	Crawls independently
_____	Crawls with assistance
_____	Does not crawl
_____	Monkey walks independently
_____	Monkey walks with assistance
_____	Does not monkey walk
_____	Crab walks independently
_____	Crab walks with assistance
_____	Does not crab walk
_____	Walks on knees independently
_____	Walks on knees with assistance
_____	Does not walk on knees
_____	Duck walks independently
_____	Duck walks with assistance
_____	Does not duck walk
_____	Can walk in wheelbarrow
_____	Cannot walk in wheelbarrow
_____	Can creep and carry peer on back
_____	Cannot creep and carry peer on back
_____	Forward rolls independently
_____	Forward rolls with assistance
_____	Does not forward roll
_____	Backward rolls independently
_____	Backward rolls with assistance
_____	Does not backward roll
_____	Headstands independently
_____	Headstands with assistance
_____	Does not headstand
_____	Cartwheels independently
_____	Cartwheels with assistance
_____	Does not cartwheel

BALANCE AND COORDINATION ACTIVITIES

Balance and coordination are, for these children, the most important componenets of the seven basic movement qualities. Three fundamental concepts apply to balance: (a) the wider the base of support, (b) the closer to the floor the body, and (c) the better the alignment of the body over the base of support, the better the balance will be. Soft landings are required. ALWAYS remain with the child, spotting, manipulating and assisting. ALWAYS do your assisting from the same position, on the same side, at the same level. Balance contributes significantly to intrasensory processing.

CHECKLIST

_____	Grasps
_____	Does not grasp
_____	Climbs up and down ladder independently
_____	Climbs up and down ladder with assistance
_____	Does not climb up and down ladder
_____	Walks inclined board independently
_____	Walks inclined board with assistance
_____	Does not walk inclined board
_____	Walks balance beam independently (2''x4'')
_____	Walks balance beam with assistance
_____	Does not walk beam
_____	Walks inclined ladder alternately independently
_____	Walks inclined ladder alternately with assistance
_____	Does not walk inclined ladder alternately
_____	Walks stepping blocks independently
_____	Walks stepping blocks with assistance
_____	Does not walk stepping blocks
_____	Walks stairs alternately independently
_____	Walks stairs alternately with assistance
_____	Does not walk stairs alternately
_____	Stands on rocking board independently
_____	Stands on rocking board with assistance
_____	Does not stand on rocking board
_____	Does not fear small base stunts
_____	Fears small base stunts

SWINGING TRAPEZE ACTIVITIES

Trapeze activities assist in improving body image, coordination, and have an element of risk. The trapeze is small, hung from a doorway or other area of the home, school, or gymnasium. A chair or stool is placed directly beneath the trapeze to assist in mounting. The teacher assists from the side, the SAME SIDE always, in helping the child. The activity affords the child, when ready, a totally new environment to deal with. Soft landing area and spotting are required.

Figure 7-2. Seat-swinging with assistance.

CHECKLIST

_____	Swings from chair independently
_____	Swings from chair with assistance
_____	Does not swing from chair
_____	Pullover independently
_____	Pullover with assistance
_____	Does not pullover
_____	Pull through independently
_____	Pull through with assistance
_____	Does not pull through
_____	Seat swings independently
_____	Seat swings with assistance
_____	Does not seat swing
_____	Hangs inverted independently

_____   Hangs inverted with assistance
_____   Does not hang inverted
_____   Hangs vertically and releases independently
_____   Hangs vertically and releases with assistance
_____   Does not hang vertically and release

DOORWAY CHINNING BAR ACTIVITIES

Pullovers, chinning and hanging (inverted or head up) are new experiences in a different mode, calling for daring and risk, as well as coordination, strength and awareness of body position. ALWAYS test the bar for weight bearing and security. Soft landings are required. Adjust the height of the bar to the height of the child.

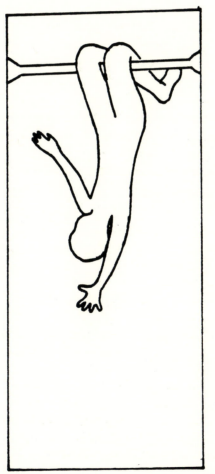

Figure 7-3. doorway chinning bar: Inverted hang.

CHECKLIST

_____	Pullover independently
_____	Pullover with assistance
_____	Does not pullover
_____	Pull through independently
_____	Pull through with assistance
_____	Does not pull through
_____	Hangs inverted independently
_____	Hangs inverted with assistance
_____	Does not hang inverted

BALL HANDLING ACTIVITIES

Ball handling is not for first-year pupils; it is too complicated for beginning teaching. Its purpose is to stimulate reaching, stopping the ball and locating the ball at the side or in front and being aware of where it is in relation to themselves. Can they track the ball with whatever hearing and vision they might have? Does the activity stimulate any residual hearing or vision present?

Use the balls in teaching about the third year. It is a higher level skill involving vision and hearing. Balls become very important when utilized by high-level functioning children, enabling them to track visually and auditorily and to hold and examine them. It is thus considered valid to include them in the program, going from lower skills to the more complex ones.

Use a hard, preferably wooden floor, to enhance the sound of the balls as they bounce or roll. Sit on the floor facing the child, with some sort of backstop behind the child.

CHECKLIST

_____	Rolls small ball
_____	Does not roll small ball
_____	Rolls medium ball
_____	Does not roll medium ball
_____	Rolls large ball
_____	Does not roll large ball
_____	Throws small ball
_____	Does not throw small ball
_____	Throws medium ball

_____	Does not throw medium ball
_____	Throws large ball
_____	Does not throw large ball
_____	Bounces ball
_____	Does not bounce ball
_____	Catches ball
_____	Does not catch ball
_____	Kicks ball
_____	Does not kick ball
_____	Strikes ball with hand
_____	Does not strike ball with hand
_____	Strikes ball with implement
_____	Does not strike ball with implement
_____	Tosses ball into box
_____	Does not toss ball into box

AQUATIC ACTIVITIES

Methods

Aquatic activities are important to deaf-blind children. The mere fact that they are introduced to a new environment will stimulate their behavior. Some will like the water at first touch, some will not. Some will grow to like it and others will like it even more. The whole point of aquatic activities and basically, for using a swimming pool, is to acquaint the youngsters with the water by doing very elementary skills similar to those done on land, i.e., walking, jumping and running. Students will perceive how different their bodies feel in the water. When there is a water program at least once a week, regularly, certain skills will be achieved that might never have been possible without the pool time. It is essentially a way to use land skills in the water.

The aquatic activities scale is a progression from water awareness to useful experiences. The child goes from self to object use when handling kickboards and hoops, balls and diving objects.

A word should be said about the method of teaching the classes. By the nature of the activity, it is a one-on-one relationship. Every child must have a teacher. It is here that the Women's Auxiliary or any volunteer organization is indispensable. These persons can be instructed as to how to proceed for the nature of the instruction is very simple. Swimming is not what is being taught; rather, dry land skills are being taught in the water. Since the pool might be used only one day a week, all the children must be in the water at once. With a teacher for each child, their behavior can be observed when they are "on their own": will they reach out, will heads go under, will they turn over, or around? How will they help themselves? All of this takes place under the watchful eye and supportive presence of the instructor.

If there is only one period a week available, always schedule the same day and time so that the child knows that there is to be swimming at that time, and looks forward to the experience. If the day is Friday, the parents look forward to this also, when they come to take their children home. Brothers and sisters can join in the activity, and it becomes a family event!

The Aquatic Activities Scale is not just an achievement scale; it is a progression in awareness and confidence. Likewise, the Aquatic Routine which follows is more than a simple list of movements; it is a repetitive, not-to-be-varied procedure to be followed in order. The child learns what is to happen, all the way from changing clothes in the locker room to the use of the hula hoop when returning to the ladder to get out. And yes, in two or three years there will be swimmers!

CHECKLIST

_____	Fears water
_____	Does not fear water
_____	Enters water by ladder independently
_____	Enters water by ladder with assistance
_____	Does not enter water by ladder
_____	Enters water with feet first jump
_____	Enters water feet first with assistance
_____	Does not enter water by feet first jump
_____	Wades in shallow water independently
_____	Wades in shallow water with assistance
_____	Does not wade in shallow water
_____	Prone floats independently
_____	Prone floats with assistance
_____	Does not prone float
_____	Prone glides independently
_____	Prone glides with assistance
_____	Does not prone glide
_____	Back floats independently
_____	Back floats with assistance

_____	Does not back float
_____	Blows bubbles
_____	Does not blow bubbles
_____	Submerges head in water
_____	Does not submerge head in water
_____	Kicks
_____	Does not kick
_____	Dog paddles
_____	Does not dog paddle
_____	Executes modified crawl stroke
_____	Does not execute modified crawl stroke
_____	Treads water
_____	Does not tread water
_____	Jumps from one meter board
_____	Does not jump from one meter board
_____	Dives into water
_____	Does not dive into water

Aquatic Routine

The aquatic routine which follows is a very important part of the experience in the swimming pool for deaf-blind children. Each trip to the pool, the routine is gone through, *without variation*. This consistency creates anticipation and gives the pupils confidence, knowing exactly what comes next. It provides a different environment for skills which they sometimes cannot learn on land. Some children who cannot walk on land can learn leg action and walk in the water. Each child has an individual teacher, preferably the same person every time.

1. Locker room (dress)
2. Enter pool area — sit on deck — feet in water
3. Enter pool backwards by the ladder
4. Acclimatize to water (teachers stand near rope)

Figure 7-4. Aquatic routine: Entering pool backwards by ladder.

5. Around the wall—across the rope (cycle)
6. Face the wall, put hands on deck, teachers move back
7. Backs to wall, elbows on deck, teachers move back
8. Back to wall, teachers lift students, give plenty of security, back out and bounce to rope, come back in
9. Face wall, teachers lift students, give plenty of security, back out and bounce to rope, come back in
10. Back to wall, fingertip control, walk students to rope and back (look for leg action)
11. Backs to wall, teacher places right hand under student's abdomen in prone position, walk to rope and back (look for leg action)
12. Face wall, put hands on edge, lift student's legs up, flutter kick assist
13. Face wall, put hands on edge, lift student's legs, shake from wall (survival reflex)
14. Face wall, put hands on deck, lift student's legs, spread apart, teacher comes between, puts students legs around waist, walk out to rope and back (arm action), take hands from abdomen on second try
15. Back to wall, give students kickboards, teachers in front pull boards out to rope and back (look for leg action)—the second time release boards
16. Face wall, teachers place one hand on chest, other under back, walk child out to rope and back (look for leg action)—second time stop in deep water, look for signs of flotation and buoyance

Figure 7-5. Aquatic routine: Assisting child on back.

17. Teachers place backs to wall, students facing them, lift child's legs up around waist, put student's back in water, walk out to rope and

back (look for arm action)

18. Face wall. Put kickboards horizontally in front of them. Lying on their backs, walk out to rope and back (look for leg action)—second time release board
19. Stand children on deck, assist feet first entry into water
20. Lift child up with back to you, make circle in deep water, bob three times, take child all the way under third time
21. The end—use large hula hoop, let child walk under hoop (submerging head), to ladder, to leave pool

Figure 7-6. Leaving pool: Heads duck under hoop to ladder.

CHAPTER EIGHT

SERVICE AND DELIVERY:
THE SCHOOL, THE PARENTS AND THE
INDIVIDUAL EDUCATIONAL PROGRAM (IEP)

WITH THE deaf-blind child, especially the severely handicapped pupil, curriculum development is presently more of an art than a science (Wilson, in Walsh and Holzberg, 1981).

The curriculum should extend from very basic skills, such as toilet training, eating and dressing; basic motor movements such as head holding, turning over, sitting upright and walking; beginning receptive and expressive language; to more advanced knowledge skills, such as the utilization of numbers and number concepts. It is incumbent upon the physical education teacher to apply all the knowledge and experience available in the field to the end that each child performs to the very highest level of ability along this continuum.

According to Public Law 94-142, there must be, in writing and approved by the IEP committee, a plan for the physical education program for each child. The physical education teacher must submit goals and objectives, both long-term and short, and a plan for assessment of each child which will indicate the activities to be used—Chapter Six of this book contains all such materials. Available instruction time coordinated with times of other teachers must be planned, and instructional units developed, with consideration of space and equipment available.

The physical education teacher should not hesitate to adapt knowledge and materials at this basic level, and include reading and numbers concepts in program plans as well as motor activities. The plan will reflect the philosophy and policy of the teacher, so it is hoped that the materials in the foregoing chapters will motivate the physical education teacher to present and carry out an effective plan. After all, the only specific course discipline mentioned in P.L. 94-142 is Physical Education. With that much emphasis, the physical educator must respond by producing an effective intervention program which will contribute to the total development of each deaf-blind child.

Competencies needed to perform tasks required of adapted physical education specialists include a wide range of roles, covering (a) Assessment and Counseling; (b) Individual Education Programming; (c) Developmental/Prescriptive Teaching and Coordination of Resources/ Services; and (d) Community Leadership/Citizen Involvement/Advocacy (Sherrill, 1986).

THE IEP CONFERENCE

The Individual Educational Program Conference is a trilogy made up of the school administrator, the teachers and the parents. Other individuals can be invited by the parents or school administrator to attend this very important conference (IEPC). It is at this IEPC that teachers and parents should take the opportunity to share with one another the concerns of how best they can reinforce what is being taught.

Parents are very important and equal members of the IEP team. Although not required to attend, it is to the benefit of both parent and child if parents participate with school personnel in all the decisions made for the deaf-blind child's educational progress. Parents have information about their child's development and needs which is important in determining the educational program. The professionals on the team may know tests and schools better than the parent, but *you, as parents, know your child.*

Active participation in the IEP Conference may be easier for parents if they come prepared. The following suggestions are designed to give an idea of the kind of information that will be valuable to the planning session (Midwest Regional Resource Center, 1983):

1. Gather together information about your child which will be helpful at the meeting. For example, medical records, copies of tests and evaluations, reports from school, and so forth.
2. If your child is already in school make an appointment to observe him/her in the classroom. Take notes on your observations.
3. Watch and record your child's behavior at home. Write down what your child can and cannot do, his/her likes and dislikes, and his/ her interactions with other children and family members.

4. Find out what your child's feelings are regarding school, home and friends.
5. Call the school and ask who will be attending the meeting. Tell the school personnel if you will be bringing a friend.
6. Notify the school personnel in advance if you will not be able to attend the meeting. Apologize for the inconvenience the change may have caused and obtain a time for another meeting.

UNDERSTANDING AND ASSISTING PARENTS IN THEIR ROLE

The role of the parent/guardian or surrogate is a highly significant one when there is a deaf-blind child in the family. Whether there are siblings or not, the parents are faced with a situation that will call for going above and beyond the call of duty. They are confronted with the establishing of attitudes that will be either wholesome or attitudes that will not be in keeping with total positive development of their deaf-blind child. On the one hand they may over-protect their deaf-blind child, and on the other hand, they may reject the child entirely. One situation is as damaging as the other. Teachers of deaf-blind children often feel that the various negative behaviors exhibited by many deaf-blind children are the result of a lack of parental interest, or a lack of stimulation when the deaf-blind child is at home, or even a lack of love and security on the parents' part. In some cases this may be true. Teachers must realize, however, that this deaf-blind child has certain negative effects on the parents that many times are very difficult to overcome.

Parents need, and more and more are asking for, help from the teacher to bridge the gap between school and home. Now that parents realize there are educational programs for their deaf-blind children, and supportive parent associations in many parts of the country, they are becoming more aware of, and fulfilling their role as parents in a most positive way. This is by no means an easy role for the parents, but support from teachers and other parents will help them in this very crucial and critical time.

Since movement is so important for the deaf-blind child, the physical education teacher should be invited to the IEPC to share with the parents a role they can play in the area of movement with their child in the home environment.

THE PARENT'S ROLE AS MOTOR SKILLS TEACHER OF THE DEAF-BLIND CHILD

When parents and other family members are at home with their children, there are many opportunities for teaching motor skills. Ordinarily, parents play with their children on an incidental basis, and perhaps do not include their deaf-blind child in these activities.

Family participation is not only possible, but can be exciting and enjoyable, once it becomes apparent that the deaf-blind child can enjoy participation with the family. When you bring your child home from school, where motor skills are taught, arrive early at the school and watch the child perform. Go to swimming class and watch your child in the water. Do some of the activities with your child, right on the spot! Then proceed with your efforts at home.

Remember that the teaching of motor skills must provide fun for the child. Fun in a child's life helps to build communication and cognitive development. Children must know who they are and where they are and what they can do with their bodies. These are necessary steps in the process of perceptual motor development.

There are five factors to employ in the cycle of teaching motor skills to deaf-blind children.

THE FIVE FACTOR CYCLE

The cycle composed of five factors can be instituted into the deaf-blind child's home environment if the parents are motivated to reinforce at home some of the motor skill activities the child is learning at school. The five factors are: (1) Plan, (2) Prescribe, (3) Teach, (4) Evaluate and (5) Reward.

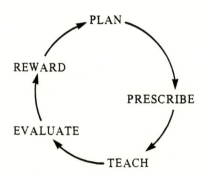

Figure 8-1. The Five Factor Cycle for teaching skills.

You PLAN the activity, just like you plan breakfast, lunch and dinner. The plan in this case is movement — movement which supplies a certain degree of muscular control and which provokes thought and creates fun.

Next you PRESCRIBE, much as your doctor gives you a prescription to take two capsules every four hours. With your child you prescribe a sequence of movements. This presciption must be at the same time and the same place and the same length of time every day.

Then you TEACH whatever activities have been prescribed. You should be able to do these activities yourself. They are not complex skills. Take yourself back to childhood days and play a role with your child as you teach these simple but important movement activities. Remember to gear your teaching to the level of your child. If your child can imitate, teach by demonstration. If you have to move your child's body with your hands, do so. To get the child to swing his leg, gently swing his leg back and forth, as you support him so he keeps his balance. Swing your own leg and let the child feel the movement. Be consistent and repeat the movement until the child can do it himself.

Now EVALUATE your child's performance. Methods of evaluation vary. A good way is to use the following scale: (1) the movement can be performed independently, (2) the movement can be performed with assistance, (3) the movement cannot be performed at present. This is an optimistic evaluation, and you need optimism!

The last factor in this cycle is REWARD. Everybody likes to know if he has done a good job. If you are a winner, you wait for the reward. So does your deaf-blind child. After your child goes through the motor skills program at home, reward him. Find some small thing to praise each time, and give social praise. You may want to keep a record of when each activity was accomplished so you can see how long it takes for him to learn it. Keep a record of the first time he walked, and when he took a ball and put it in a box, or handed you a toy. The child may forget, so go back and start again.

Examples of Activities That Can be Taught at Home

Examples of activities that can be taught by the five factor cycle are:

Movement Activities

1. Log roll
2. Scoot forward

   3. Scoot backward
   4. Creep or crawl
   5. Knee walk
   6. Monkey walk
   7. Crab walk forward
   8. Crab walk backward
   9. Forward roll
 10. Back roll
 11. Headstand
 12. Ride your parent's back

EVALUATION OF ACTIVITIES

Use a sheet of paper with the following data, possibly with dates when each activity is accomplished, and how.

EVALUATION SHEET

Name: _____

Dates: _____

+ = independently
0 = with assistance
− = cannot do at present

_____	1. Log roll	_____	7. Crab walk forward
_____	2. Scoot forward	_____	8. Crab walk backward
_____	3. Scoot backward	_____	9. Forward roll
_____	4. Creep or crawl	_____	10. Backward roll
_____	5. Knee walk	_____	11. Headstand
_____	6. Monkey walk	_____	12. Ride Daddy (smiles)

Just remember to KEEP UP THE GOOD WORK! It will pay off.

As we end this book we have just learned of the passage of P.L. 99-457, the *Early Childhood Amendment,* which mandates in all states, by the school year 1991, education for handicapped children ages birth through three years. This will require movement and motor experience intervention at even an earlier age than at the present time. The role of the physical education teacher has become so important now in helping remediate motor problems that the material presented in this book generates a renewed interest and hope for parents and children alike that may have been identified as handicapped.

BIBLIOGRAPHY

1. Ayres, A. Jean: SENSORY INTEGRATION AND LEARNING DISOR-DERS. Los Angeles, Western Reserve Psychological Services, 1972.
2. Bladergroen, Wilhelmina J.: "The Body Image in Relation to the Physical Education of the Pre-Lingually Deaf Child." The Netherlands, State University of Gronigen.
3. Freeman, Peggy: UNDERSTANDING THE DEAF-BLIND CHILD. London, Wm. Heinemann Medical Books Ltd., 1975. pp. 4,1, Chapters 1-5.
4. Magin, Kevin: "Movement-based Language: The van Dijk Model." Lansing, Michigan Department of Education, 1980.
5. Midwest Regional Resource Center: "A Parent's Guide to Special Education in Missouri." Des Moines, 1983. (Pamphlet).
6. Myklebust, Helmer R.: THE PSYCHOLOGY OF DEAFNESS, 2nd ed. New York, Grune, 1964. pp. 45-50, 224, 225.
7. Piaget, Jean: THE LANGUAGE AND THOUGHT OF THE CHILD. New York, World Publishing, 1955.
8. Sherrill, Claudine: ADAPTED PHYSICAL EDUCATION AND RECREA-TION, 3rd. ed. Dubuque, Brown, 1986. pp. 272, 616, 617.
9. Smithdas, Robert J: "Psychological Aspects of Deaf-Blindness." A paper prepared for presentation at the Convention of World Federation of the Deaf, Sands Point, Helen Keller National Center for Deaf-Blind Youths and Adults, 1975.
10. Southwest Regional Deaf-Blind Center: LEARNING STEPS. Sacramento, California State Department of Education, 1976.
11. Thielman, Virginia; Myer, Sandra; Lowell, Edgar: CORRESPONDENCE LEARNING PROGRAM FOR PARENTS OF PRE-SCHOOL DEAF-BLIND CHILDREN. Los Angeles, John Tracy Clinic, 1973.
12. van Dijk, Jan: "Motor Development in the Education of Deaf-Blind Children." Paper presented at the Conference on Deaf-Blind, Holland, St. Michielsgestel, 1965.
13. Walsh, Sara R., and Holzberg, Robert, eds.: UNDERSTANDING AND EDU-CATING THE DEAF-BLIND/SEVERELY AND PROFOUNDLY HANDI-CAPPED. Springfield, Thomas, 1981. pp. 35, 36, 73-75, 134.
14. Williams, Harriet G.: PERCEPTUAL AND MOTOR DEVELOPMENT. Englewood Cliffs, Prentice-Hall, 1983. Chapters 5 and 6.

OTHER REFERENCES

1. "A Glossary of the Eye." Columbus, Ohio Rehabilitation Services Commission, (pamphlet).
2. Anderson, Harry C.: "Usher's Syndrome: Questions and Answers." St. Augustine, Office of Demographic and Vocational Potential for the Deaf-Blind.
3. Black, Dolores A.: "Suggested Learning Activities for Body Image and Posture." Unpublished paper. Bowling Green, Bowling Green State University.
4. "Deaf-Blind Resource Materials," revised edition. Watertown, New England Regional Center for Services to Deaf-Blind Children, 1981, (list).
5. Esche, Jean and Griffin, Carol: "A Handbook for Parents of Deaf-Blind Children." Lansing, Michigan School for the Blind (pamphlet).
6. Hagerty, Joyce Smoot: "Three Hundred Success Play Materials/Equipment/ Activities Checklist for Deaf-Blind Children." Lansing, Mid-West Regional Center for Service to Deaf-Blind Children (list).
7. de Leuw, Lieke: "Exceptional Disorders in the Language Acquisition of Deaf-Blind and Multiply Handicapped Deaf Children." Paris, European Conference for Education of Deaf-Blind Children, 1970.
8. Rudolph, James M.; Bjorling, Barbara; and Collins, Michael T.: "Assessment of a Deaf-Blind Multiply Handicapped Child," 3rd ed. Lansing, Michigan Department of Education (manual).
9. Scholl, Geraldine T.: FOUNDATIONS-OF-EDUCATION FOR BLIND AND VISUALLY IMPAIRED HANDICAPPED CHILDREN AND YOUTHS. New York, American Foundation for the Blind, 1986.
10. "The Pre-school Deaf-Blind Child." New York, American Foundation for the Blind (pamphlet).
11. Tierney, Paula: "Co-Active Movement and the Deaf-Blind Child." Lansing, Michigan Department of Education.
12. Tutt, Louis M.: Videotapes of Motor Skills Development With Deaf-Blind Children at the Michigan School for the Blind, St. Louis, Missouri School for the Blind, 1973.
13. van Dijk, Jan: "Movement and Communication with Rubella Children." Address given at the National Association for Deaf-Blind and Rubella Children Annual General Meeting, May 6th, The Netherlands, St. Michielsgestel, 1968.
14. _____: "The Non-Verbal Blind Child and His World: His Outgrowth Toward the World of Symbols." The Netherlands, St. Michielsgestel, 1967.
15. Walker, Barbara: "Challenge for Parents." Arlington, Texas National Association for Parents of Visually Impaired Children, 1986.
16. Webster, Richard: THE ROAD TO FREEDOM, A PARENT'S GUIDE TO PREPARE THE BLIND CHILD TO TRAVEL INDEPENDENTLY. Jacksonville, Katan Publications, 1977.
17. Werner, H., and Kaplan, B.: SYMBOL FORMATION, New York, Wiley, 1963.

INDEX